Family By Choice
Platonic Partnered Parenting

Rachel Hope

ISBN: 0615946275
ISBN-13: 978-0615946276

DEDICATION

Family By Choice: Platonic Partnered Parenting is dedicated to all the children who are my family. Each child's unique and exuberant style of growing up in a family by choice has affirmed the heart and purpose of this book.

iv

CONTENTS

Acknowledgments

This book is like a baby I have incubated for over half my life. Countless people have asked me to tell them why, how, and with whom they should create a partnered family. In these pages I have done my best to answer their questions.

Producers, reporters, TV hosts, critics, and researchers from all over the world have been a driving force behind the creation of this book in the last year. In response to the thousands of people now looking for a parenting partner, these media people turned to me for answers. The TV interviews and magazine articles have been appreciated, but because of time and space constraints much of the realities and details of Partnered Parenting have been lost. This book will complete the picture.

Who helped make this "baby" book? The profound love and familial bond with my parenting partners Glenn Pierce and Paul Wenner is the foundation for *Family By Choice*. As with my own late father, Roger Benson, these fathers have taught me how love and devotion are like shock absorbers on the bumpiest of roads.

My two biological children, Jesse Pierce and Grace Hope, are different people in every way. One was conceived naturally; the other by advanced reproductive science. One was a homebirth with a midwife and the other was born in a state-of-the-art hospital. One child is mellow, shy and methodical; the other is wildly expressive, social, and imaginative. Parenting these children born 18 years apart has made me a vulnerable and curious mom.

This book was also inspired by the many children that have come to live with me, sometimes for days and often for years. Most of them came to me in states of crises, from broken homes and lives. Although all of them have extraordinary resilience and courage, it was heartbreaking to see how the conventional family system failed them. I hope the information in this book helps new families to form environments for their children to thrive and be nurtured into healthy, happy adults.

It takes a village! Other essential members of the team that have brought this book to life are the following:

Mitchell Sisskind, who has organized and edited this book through its numerous drafts. He is the reason these ideas are readable. He is your champion, dear reader.

Marcus Brown spent over a year making our family, computers and businesses work while also scheduling a blur of interviews between my manic writing episodes. With gifts of intuition he helped make our complicated family function. He also has the technical computer skills to administer my website, PartneredParentingMagazine.com, and get this book through the publishing process, and much more. He is family by choice.

Joe Straczynski has been my guide and inspiration. He has been the most generous and professionally savvy person I have ever met. With his decades of experience on the cutting edge of new social ideas, his validation of Partnered Parenting has convinced me its time has come.

Dr. Pat Allen has been my teacher and mentor for over 27 years. Much of this book has been directly inspired by her work as a cognitive, behavioral, and child and family therapist. Through her books, seminars, and live presentations, I have been imprinted with her heartfelt stoicism.

The efforts and generosity of Chris Russell, Sid Cronin, David Tiktin, Gregory Arthur, Mark Gould, Curtis Hannum, Joe Williamson, Alan Harrison and Rick Leeks have added key ingredients in the creation of this book. When I was at a breaking point, one of these daddy-heroes would pay one of my bills, care for a child, do my errands, or make a meal just in time to keep my cause and hope alive.

Renee Eisenman, Bob Levitan, Jaclyn Easton, and Len Rosen have provided far more than exceptional professional services. They made me look good, sound smart, have a web presence and helped me tell my story over and over again. They gave this book a pulse.

My mother, Megan Wells, and my 91 year-old grandmother, Ruth Wells, taught me to stick to core values and beliefs, no matter how unpopular. Harbingers of fifty years ago, they were considered weird woman doing yoga and eating whole foods. Now these practices are everywhere, and they are likely the reason I have the fertility of a 32 year-old and the energy of a 22 year-old at the age of 42!

I love to stun people by saying, "A beautiful Chinese-American woman impregnated me….with Grace." The woman's name is Dr. Wendy Chang, and she is one of the exceptionally talented doctors at Southern California Reproductive Center. Without Dr. Chang and the other brilliant staff at SCRC we would not have our Gracie girl. I recently took part in a panel discussion at SCRC, where my message of Partnered Parenting was enthusiastically received.

Ivan Fatovic of Modamily.com has been supportive in helping me find my next parenting partner and giving me many opportunities to tell the world my story. Ivan is the grand facilitator and matchmaker for the growing community of partnered parents. Keep an eye on this guy!

Lastly, I thank my future parenting partner(s) for drawing me forward. My desire to realize my dream of at least two more biological children as well as several other foster and adoptive children is all-consuming. As I write this, I have not made my final choices and arrangements for my next partnered parent, but all my candidates are wonderful, qualified, and will make excellent fathers. My plan is to be pregnant by the end of 2014. In affirmation of this, I say thank you for being the counterpart of a dream coming true and a destiny fulfilled!

I offer this book as the first and only one of its kind. May it serve as the roadmap for happy and sustainable modern families. This will also be the guidebook for my continued speaking and coaching services, God willing.

Your reading this book now means it has been born this moment. Let it speak for itself -- but without waiting until the age of three!

One: What is Partnered Parenting?

Partnered Parenting refers to a variety of possible arrangements in which the parents are not in a marital or romantic relationship with one another. Partnership parenting may be chosen by individuals who are seeking to have children, but who do not wish to enter into a conventional relationship. Such arrangements may come into being in many ways. For example, parenting partnerships can be established between lifelong friends, or by new acquaintances that are discovered online or through other media.

My apologies if the paragraph above seems a bit dry, but I hope it at least defines the term "Partnered Parenting." With that definition as a starting point, this book is about determining if you are a good candidate for Partnered Parenting; finding a good parenting match; forming a parenting partnership agreement; and creating a great custom-designed family.

These are things I've learned from my two greatly successful experiences with partnered families over a 23 year period. Partnered Parenting is a social evolution and an answer to many modern concerns about avoiding divorce, racing a biological clock, and having a family when you're ready even if you've not yet met your soul mate. I believe this social evolution is ultimately heading toward a revival of our ancestors' traditions of living and parenting as a small tribe of people who cooperated for a better life. A major part of this cooperation was the advantage of sharing the responsibility of protecting, providing for, and raising children.

Summer 2013, Maui, Hawaii. Rachel with her
son Jesse, 22, and her daughter Grace, 4.

Over the course of history so many different
societies and civilizations have come and gone.
They've been organized in every imaginable way.

There have been patriarchies, matriarchies, monarchies, democracies. But amid all these differences, there has been one common thread: "Be fruitful, and multiply, and replenish the earth." This verse, from the first chapter of the Bible, is ostensibly spoken by God but the thought also comes from somewhere deep within the human spirit. It expresses an innate urge within our species to have and raise children.

It's important to note, however, that this urge applies to the human species as a whole. Specific individuals may feel differently, just as individuals can feel differently about any other human inclination. The choice of whether to parent children or not is obviously a basic right, and it may be the most basic right of all. People's choices in this area should not only be recognized, but also honored.

I am one of the people who yearn with all my heart and soul to bring children into the world, to guide them and care for them. I am confident that readers of this book feel the same way. We share a connection with the primordial urge referenced in that Biblical verse. We want to be parents.

Within that basic desire, all sorts of variations are possible – many more than we might assume from looking at only the United States or Western Europe. And even within that very limited area, whole new universes of family designs are coming into being. This fact, and this freedom, is bringing the possibility of parenthood to literally millions of people who might have been excluded in the past. Thanks to scientific advances that no one could have imagined a generation ago, virtually anyone in the 21st century who sincerely wants to be a parent can and should be one – provided they can fulfill the very serious responsibilities that parenthood entails.

This book is a brief introduction to a very wide-ranging topic. In these pages you will find the information you need to become a parenting partner.

Two: Who am I?

I was born in Southern California, but I lived for almost twenty years in Hawaii. That's where I raised my son in my first, Partnered Parenting relationship. Now I'm back in California raising my daughter in another parenting partnership.

November 1990, Maui, Hawaii. Glenn and Rachel, pregnant with Jesse.

I've done many different things over the years. In the late 1980's, for instance, I became an environmental activist. While lecturing in high schools and middle schools in California, New York, New Jersey, and Canada, I learned a few things about how young people saw their future. Often, I was the same age as my audience, and we shared the same dreams.

In a global sense, we dreamed of a thriving planet where happy, healthy lives could be lived and families could be raised. As individuals, the youth of my era intended to become educated and experienced before picking a partner and having children. Like good ecologists, they wanted their families to be sustainable and their marital love perennial. They didn't want the divorces and broken homes of their parents. The confusion, liberation, and social revolutions of the 60's and 70's gave permission to question and even rebel against the status quo. But as it turned out, the broken families left in the wake of these lofty dreams were just as numerous as what came before. Marriages that began during and after this turbulent period are still failing in very large numbers.

Many men and women now in their 30s and 40s thought that having kids later in life, with the benefit of education and real world experience, would insulate them from divorce. So they waited. Then some paired up, but some of those had waited too long. Many are now dealing with issues of age-related infertility that must be overcome in family planning facilities. Others were and are clearly outside the definition of conventional relationships — Lesbian, Gay, Bisexual, Transgender (LGBT) or polyamorous lifestyles — which requires some real innovation in order to responsibly start a family.

My generation was called "Generation X." Were we slackers, or just taking our time, trying to avoid "haste makes waste?" Along the way some of us became professionals, activists, leaders, advocates, addicts, single parents, or lonely outsiders. But did we invent new ways of living, or just alienate ourselves from tradition?

Whatever we did, there is one element that could make even the messiest situations and the biggest mistakes turn out well. That element is *responsibility*. If we take full responsibility for what we do and for how we affect others, we can recycle and renew our past in every area of life, including the creation of Partnered Parenting families. We can make conscientiously designed families an extension of our truly unique selves.

None of this can happen by itself, but it *can* happen. Glenn, my parenting partner with our son, was different from me in many ways and we certainly deviated from the standard "couple" template. We agreed from the start that I would be the principal earner while Glenn assumed more of the stay-at-home responsibilities. We also shared some very strong beliefs. We didn't want to be in unstable marriages like our parents and step-parents. We wanted more sustainable parenting for our child. By dealing with our issues at the outset and by adhering to our principles, we didn't need to keep asking, "Is this working for us?" Our son Jesse flourished and so did we.

Paul is my second parenting partner. At the age of 60, he thought he'd never have children. In 2007 Paul's dream of having a daughter was almost forgotten. When he agreed to become my known donor and a hands-on parenting partner, his dream unexpectedly came true. But Paul never had to give up his autonomous life and dedication to his work. As a partnered parent, he became a father without signing on to the complexities and risks of marriage.

As I write this, I am in regular contact with one other Partnered Parenting family. My friends Cindy and Will are brother and sister co-parents. Cindy used donor sperm to become pregnant with Ella. She planned to be a single mother with a loving and supportive family. She had some serious challenges and health concerns during her pregnancy that made single motherhood impossible. Her brother Will stepped up and became "Uncle Daddy" to Ella, and the family has been meeting these challenges together.

Cindy waited to have kids until the ticking clock created a now-or-never situation. Will gave himself to being a parent in spite of his lifestyle of a single gay man. These people are social innovators for the love of Ella. This is a lovely example of a custom family design with the freedom of social innovation. They have a sustainable family. As a gay man, Will might never have had children, but I know that Ella's world, as well as our community of Los Angeles, is better off because of the way things have turned out.

Paul, Grace, and I have a sustainable home life not because we have the ideal ingredients, but because we make the best of the ingredients we have. We are free of the romantic expectations that so often reduce families to broken parts destined for the scrap heap.

Three: Are you ready to be a parent?

Many people just feel ready to be parents, and that feeling is one good indicator that they _are_ ready. But just as a seed is not yet a plant, a feeling cannot be the sole indicator of true readiness.

There are many factors in determining if you are ready: financial stability, time, residence, emotional maturity, and above all having a parenting partner.

I once had a teacher tell me, "Vague questions get vague answers." After 23 years of contemplating and discussing this topic, I have simplified the inquiry of parenting readiness into just two questions. Sincere exploration of these questions will lead you to much self-discovery and clarification of your true intentions. Here are two essential questions of readiness for parenting:

-- Is it in the best interests of the child to be born to you and your parenting partner at this time and place?

-- Is it in the best interests of the community and the world for you to have a child at this time and place with your parenting partner?

It might be good to talk with a professional counselor when answering these two questions. For now, I hope in this chapter you'll discover more about your core motivations and values. From here you can begin to make a list of questions for yourself.

Questions I ask myself as I prepare to pick my next parenting partner, and have my third child, are:

1. What are the resources, skills, and experience I will contribute to my child and my parenting partner?

Some of my answers are: my assets and earning ability; my flexibility and willingness to renegotiate with kindness and respect; and my experience raising children, including my oldest biological child - conceived and raised start to finish - in a co-parenting agreement.

2. Why do I believe that I will be a good parent?

I know what it's like to be parented by people who were not ready to be parents. I am totally committed to doing it differently for my children. This includes seeking out and learning from parents whom I respect.

3. What qualities will make a good parenting partner for you?

I look for someone with a track record of making and keeping agreements. My first parenting partner had few financial resources, but he was impeccable with his word. I felt that we could build on his reliability. My teacher Dr. Pat Allen says, "The only way you can know how much love anyone has is by the agreements they make and keep."

Paul, my second co-parent, shares my core value of making the world a better place. I am an environmental activist, and his life's purpose is to make the world a better place by providing healthy, natural food products including GardenBurger and GardenBar. We are complementary in the way we parent. He is very attentive in teaching our daughter practical skills, and I am good at creating travel adventures and a rich social life for her.

Determining your own readiness for parenthood, as well as the readiness of potential partners, are very big subjects. I hope you will share your thoughts and questions so we can begin to develop reliable self-awareness and a clearer understanding of what being ready for parenting means to us.

Four: Are you ready to be a *partnered* parent?

Please give careful attention to each of the questions in this section, and also ask someone who knows you well to answer the questions about _you_. It's a good idea to write your answers in a journal that can serve as a resource when you interview prospective matches.

The journal will be helpful in sharing the development of your intentions and plans for your future children. Someday your journal could even become a gift to your child when he or she is ready to plan a family.

There are no right or wrong answers to these questions, but completely honest responses will help you discover the style of parenting and family that's best for you. You may find that the answers you give now are different from what you might have written in the past. If so, note that down. Try to explain when and how the changes took place.

>> Is finding a parenting partner your first choice, or is it Plan B if -- for whatever reason -- another option did not work out? Have you experienced grief in the process of adjusting to the loss of a dream? Or, are you now first learning about Partnered Parenting and thinking "I've always been looking for a way to have my family just like this! This fits what I really want and now I know the option exists."

>> Do you have strong feelings of possessiveness for the things, people, and relationships you value most? Do you feel a need to guard and maintain exclusivity with your car, house, close friends, love interests? Did you have intense sibling rivalries when you were growing up? Did you compete for your parents' attention, or for academic or athletic accomplishments? Or do you feel a desire and even a need to have other people share in your experiences, even the most personal ones? Do you encourage your loved ones to have strong relationships with others and take joy in this? Do you easily share your possessions with trusted companions and family?

>> On a scale from 1 to 10, rate yourself for jealously. One being almost never feeling that someone else threatens your connections to what and who you value and

10 is feeling an almost daily threat to most of your relationships and activities.

>> What aspects of your family of origin and/or your experiences growing up might prepare you for Partnered Parenting? On the other hand, what experiences might make Partnered Parenting a challenge for you?

>> Can you devote at least 12 months to really getting to know a future parenting partner? Developing the relationship ought to include weekly meetings for continuity, and frequent phone calls and emails. This is a project that will require real diligence, and sufficient time for that diligence to take place.

>> Can you name at least three friends or family members who will be providing support to you and your partnered family? Describe how they have been supportive in the past,

and what you feel they will do to contribute to your raising a child in the future. Also, are you aware of anyone who you believe will create a challenge to your forming an alternative family? What experiences give you this impression? How will you deal with this negative presence?

>> How long have you been independently responsible for yourself? When did you move away from home, and when did you become financially self-sufficient? If you are still relying on others to meet your needs, will those people be a committed part of your family? Will their resources be extended to your children and for how long? Will they sign legal contracts to this effect?

>> Rate your level of self-care from one to ten. A rating of one means you have serious difficulties keeping yourself, fed, fit, and emotionally balanced. Ten means you

consistently meet all your personal needs and feel confident that you can do so indefinitely. Self-care involves several different categories of personal experience including: physical needs such as nutrition, rest, bathing, fitness, medicine, grooming, and sex; meaningful and appropriate expression of emotions, image, and the recognition and exchange of these feelings with others; maintaining significant bonds that last through difficulties, as well as regular contact with new and interesting people; and a sense of connection to the world as a whole, through spiritual, political, or citizenship practices. After assigning a number to each category briefly describe the basis for the number.

>> What is your experience and comfort level with children? What has been the age range of the kids you've been around, and in what settings has this taken place? How is your comfort level regarding dirt, diapers, and

messes of all sizes and kinds? Have you ever had an experience of prolonged sleep deprivation? How did this affect you?

>> What background, abilities, resources, experience and ideology do you have that will match and harmonize with a unique and customized family life?

>> What experience do you have in discussing and explaining non-traditional ideas to people who are unfamiliar with them? What is your comfort and patience level answering questions and concerns regarding alternative families and lifestyles? Do you feel annoyed and frustrated, or do you feel like an educator and pioneer?

>> Have you created or tried to create a family with someone in the past? What was the outcome? How might this affect your perspective on building a family now? Do you

feel there are any unresolved issues regarding this experience? If you have children, how would you describe your relationship with them?

>> With regard to core values such as religion or the absence of it, are you able to coexist with others who believe differently than you? How will you explain the world to your children? Do you want them to believe as you do, or figure things out for themselves? Do you feel responsible for changing the way others close to you believe about the world? Or, are you relaxed about differing beliefs?

>> What role do you imagine yourself playing as a partnered parent? Would you divide all the responsibilities equally such as child care, finances, chores, planning, and so forth. Or would you specialize as a primary care giver or provider? Are you more interested in "hands-on" parenting a baby or small child

until school age, and then going back to work? Or would you want the primary childcare to go to a nanny or to the other parent while you focus on your career?

Spring 2008. Grace and Rachel on the train to Santa Barbara, California, for work.

Five: Learning from your self-assessment

Answering the questions from the previous chapter should be the first step in knowing where you stand with regard to Partnered Parenting. The second step is to understand what your answers really mean. What did you learn about yourself? Did you answer the questions in a journal for future reference? If not, that's okay -- but be aware that the level of clarity and focus you have before you become a parent will be reflected in the choices you make and affect the outcome for your family and children.

I had also suggested that you ask someone else to answer the questions as if the questions were about _you_. Were you able to do this? What did you learn from that person's answers? Did anything surprise you?

Readiness and willingness for Partnered Parenting can't be fully determined by answering a few questions in a book. But there are certain elements that can definitely be useful indicators. Here are some thoughts on what I feel should (and should not) be present in your self-assessment.

The first question, for example, asked whether Partnered Parenting is your first choice for designing a family, or is it an alternative to another possibility that did not work out. This may seem like a loaded question, but it really isn't. Even if it isn't your Plan A, Partnered Parenting can still work beautifully as your Plan B. The important thing is to know how you see it, and to let go of any previous plans in order to successfully create a partnered family life.

Of course, you are also free to change your mind about a parenting partnership right up until you sign the legal agreements. If and when you do choose to sign those agreements, be sure about your choice. Don't sidetrack someone else's dreams by not being fully prepared to keep your commitments.

While the details of parenting partnerships can take many forms, there is one absolute certainty: _sharing_ is always the foundation. The ability to share easily and naturally is the key, because offering your time, energy, and resources to your family members is of benefit to yourself in the long run. It's self-interest in the best sense of the term.

When I say that sharing should be done naturally, that doesn't mean it will always be easy. Possessiveness, which we can define as the opposite of sharing, is a very powerful force. I don't intend to demonize it here. I believe possessiveness has its roots in evolutionary psychology and expresses a drive to "mate guard" and to retain goods and resources. In some important ways this has served humanity and advanced civilization. A possessive impulse can be extremely useful for recognizing and warding off intruders and thieves of all kinds, who could break up a family for purely selfish reasons. On the other hand, possessive feelings should not lead you to block others from connecting with your loved ones, nor should you be cut off because of someone else's possessiveness.

Jealously is a specific form of possessiveness that most likely has an evolutionary basis. My preferred definition of jealousy is "a perceived threat to a valued relationship." The word _threat_ is important, because its connotation of violence implies the dangerous turn that jealousy can take. Possessiveness in many forms can cause difficulty, but jealousy is especially problematic because it's deeply rooted in our biochemistry. It's a very strong feeling that can surprise us with its suddenness and its force.

Have you had strong feelings of jealousy in past relationships? Do you believe that a platonic parenting arrangement will automatically allow you to escape those feelings? If so, this is a mistaken assumption. The instinctual bond with a child is profound, and many people experience jealousy even toward the child's other loved ones.

Perceiving another parent, a grandparent, a teacher, or any other well-meaning individual as a threat can be destructive. It can undermine your sense that "we're all on the same team." It can subvert your ability to act in the best interests of your child.

If jealously is an issue for you, try to replace it with a sense of personal joy in the happiness your child finds with others. Instead of feeling that someone is threatening your special bond, focus on ways that other people can help you cultivate the happiness and success you all desire for your child. Rest assured that you can never be replaced. There is only one you.

Coming from a serene, high functioning family of origin can of course be a great foundation for Partnered Parenting. Sadly, many of us do not come from such a background, but people from all kinds of families can be great partnered parents. If you had a difficult or even a destructive family of origin, Partnered Parenting can be an alternative and a protection against the unconscious replications that so many people fall into. If you are building a custom designed family, you will consciously avoid the mistakes you saw as you grew up, rather than simply falling into them by default. You will also benefit from having the complex dynamics of sex and romance removed from the family equation.

Family experience is useful for creating a partnered family, but it can also be a mold you have to break out of too. It is important not to carry psychological baggage from a previous domestic situation into a new, custom family. Try to let go of expectations. Focus on what you want to create now. This is what you and your partner have agreed upon.

So much conflict in conventional families is about sex, money, and in-laws. If you have these topics clearly negotiated in a legal contract, there will be far less cause for strife. There will of course be problems and conflicts, but Partnered Parenting is built on finding solutions and moving forward. Compared to traditional families, however, a partnered family includes far fewer preconceived assumptions and expectations about what mothers and fathers should be and should do.

In no particular order, here are some further observations based on the self-assessment questions....

***

Time influences every aspect of human life, and this certainly includes family life of all kinds. I believe that getting to know a potential parenting partner with whom you're not previously acquainted requires at least 12 months. If you're not able to devote that much time, you might want to pick someone from your circle of family and friends and start a new courtship. Geography is also crucial as you explore Partnered Parenting. You've got to grow a tree and build a nest before you lay any eggs. At the very least, you should know where you intend to live and know that the location is agreeable to your potential partner.

***

Making a basic assessment of your finances and earning ability is important in your self-evaluation. If you have provided for yourself over many years and clearly have the means to support others, than go for it. If not, some planning is in order. Saving money, lowering expenses, and/or finding a partner who can be take primary financial responsibility are all good options. Making some necessary adjustments before you start looking for a parenting partner might make your situation more attractive. A savings account, hard assets, and life insurance are some things to consider.

***

Are there areas of your life in which you feel unsure of your knowledge and judgment? Seek guidance in those areas from people you admire. It's tempting to invest time and energy where you already feel competent, but this just leads to imbalance. For instance, if you love your career but have a crisis in a relationship, you might want to escape into your work to avoid it. It may seem counter-intuitive to go to the gym instead, but going in a new direction can be liberating and even enlightening.

***

I know a few people who are seriously horrified by "yuck." This is a major obstacle to having children, which involves plenty of "yuck." There is no way to escape this, so be honest with yourself. Helping to care for kids in your extended family or in your neighborhood can provide insight and experience. You may find that the reality of "yuck" is less horrifying than the idea of it!

***

If you are a person who does not fit neatly into the conventions and expectations of mainstream society, you have a head start in being ready for

Partnered Parenting -- and also for helping others get ready. As you go forward with your parenting partnership, you can draw on your experience to counsel those who are less familiar with this new concept of family. Moreover, as you become comfortable in speaking about your family, your kids will be listening. You'll be teaching them how to talk about your alternative family with knowledge and confidence.

***

Complacency or neutrality are not elements of a solid parenting partnership. Passions and opinions make us the kind of vital, energetic human beings who can be good parents. Strive to find someone whose core values match yours, but different religions, political beliefs, or even ideas about parenting are not necessarily deal breakers. What's really essential is peaceful coexistence with your differences, and a commitment to your child's well-being as the highest value.

Six: Parenting Partners - finding them and "courting"

I found my two parenting partners among my family and friends. If you're also able to do that, you'll have the advantage of some shared personal history. You'll feel like you're taking less of a risk than you would with a new connection. This can be a bit misleading. However, a relationship in one context doesn't necessarily translate to another. So take a fresh look at everyone you consider for Partnered Parenting.

Get the word out to your friends, work associates, neighbors, and everyone else who you think might be able to help. Don't be secretive about your desire to create a partnered family, because you'll get free "advertising" from the interest your plan will generate. Parenting classes and lectures on parenting and fertility are other good opportunities. The LGBT community and their support groups are tried and true.

Becoming a foster parent is an outstanding way to make connections with people who are learning to parent as teammates with others. I received foster parent training three times, and it's been invaluable to my success in family life. This will give you a clear sense of what parenting is really like (if you don't have kids already) and it's a major gift to society and our community's children. As a foster parent, you're part of a team comprised of social workers, therapists, teachers, and possibly the birth family of the children. The skills and knowledge you'll need for a parenting partnership will rapidly develop. Of these skills, the most important is knowing how to put the best interests of your children first. This will be the common goal of all your teammates in caring for your foster child. Another advantage to foster parenting is the personal and support group connections you make and develop. This can facilitate the possibility of adopting the foster child in your care, should he or she be eligible.

Occasionally I've come across online postings or articles about people looking for a parenting partner before the websites existed. A gay man, for example, wrote about his search in a widely circulated magazine. When I contacted him, I learned that he wanted to find a woman who was already pregnant and "abandoned." He wanted to put his name to the birth certificate and then actively assume the role of the child's father. He felt this plan would do more good for more people than if he chose to be a biological father. I certainly supported this, and wished him well. I was also impressed that he'd written an article to go after what he wanted. I've been using the same strategy. I've appeared in almost every media spot that I've been offered, in hopes of broadening my exposure and options.

I've also noticed people who create blogs related to their search. Then they drive traffic to those blogs, which act as vivid advertisement of who they are and what they're seeking. Facebook pages can serve the same purpose. Facebook can also be a quick way of making connections from your schools, neighborhoods, and other past associations.

Using the internet to find parenting partners is obviously essential, but it's also important to get out from behind your computer and meet people face to face. Most large cities have meet-up events for would-be parents, especially for people in the LGBT community, and for those seeking fertility medicine and third party donors. Attending presentations and meet-ups lets you connect with many people at once and can save time compared to making individual dates. Modamily.com currently hosts events in Los Angeles and New York and will likely be adding more locations soon.

You can also start your own meet-up group based

on alternative parenting, alternative family, family planning, fertility medicine, surrogacy, egg and sperm donation, open adoptions, foster parenting, LGBT parenting, or anything else that will foster connections. The key is making a commitment to organize and hold monthly events for at least six months. Mixing kid-friendly and family events along with adults-only meetings is a good idea. Don't form a group of childless people to talk about wishing to have a child. Be a group that's part of a community of families and prospective families.

With the help of social media, festivals like Burning Man and Joshua Tree are full of people who are interested in new approaches to relationships, family formations, and community life. These are your people. Websites, such as Festival Chaser and Fest 300, list and describe these festivals. Do a web search for your area and consider visiting festivals that could help you make valuable connections.

At Burning Man 2013 I saw a sandwich board that a

woman had put up, detailing the kind of parenting partner she was looking for. The board included her location at the festival and her email address. This was a low- tech but effective way for thousands of people to learn about her search.

I had three different people tell me about her sign. Festival culture is the ultimate in social networking with a pulse rather than a computer keyboard.

The search for a parenting partner can be time consuming, but think of it as the first step in your new life as a parent. Your efforts also help to expand the social innovation of Partnered Parenting. By broadening awareness, you create more options for others and help prepare the world for your unique family. This builds legitimacy for your future children to enjoy.

***

Parenting "courtship" is an adventure. Like dating, it begins with an exchange with a stranger or strangers via a social gathering, online, and/or on the phone. But once rapport has been established for the purpose of "getting to know each other," co-parenting courtship focuses on more practical issues than conventional dating.

The interview process usually starts with less small talk and more direct and deep questions than we're used to in casual social interactions. I think this is a good sign, since we are looking for people who are really concerned with and invested in their future child's well-being.

Spring 1990, California, Glenn and Rachel sizing each other up.

The best co-parenting courtship practices require a significant investment of time and effort. But that investment will translate into an even more significant salvation from heartache and disappointment. In other words, we're going to be looking at some very useful information – and all of it has been tested by me, validated by child and family therapists, and endorsed by fellow trailblazers.

A key step is courting people who really want to be in a parenting partnership. You can begin to see clues about this early on. If people are unreliable about keeping phone appointments or plans to meet, you can expect the same thing in their parenting style. Conversely, when people walk their talk at the start, there's reason to believe they'll do that all the way through.

***

The first date should take place after emails or phone calls have shown enough potential to justify a meeting. Why you are seeking this type of family? What resources and abilities can you contribute to a partnered family life? These are some questions that should come up as soon as possible. If satisfactory responses are forthcoming, an informal coffee date can be the next step. This should last about an hour, and not more than an hour and a half. If you want to keep courting, agree on another date when you'll discuss how often to see each other. After a month or so, there should be a face-to-face meeting at least every other week. If you can't do it in person, you should use FaceTime or Skype.

Taking turns as initiator and planner is a good idea. Some good activities include recreational sports like bowling, casual dinner parties and socializing with diverse groups of friends, and visits to each other's homes. See where your possible partners live, and also _how_ they live. Of course, spending time with kids together is very important too.

***

Some candidates will show up at a date with a file showing their medical history and sperm count. They're ready to start talking about insemination. Others will act like they're on a romantic date, opening doors, paying the check, bringing flowers, complimenting you on your "good genes." Some might come from work in a uniform. Others will be dressed like they were mowing the yard and just stopped by for a quick cup of coffee. On some of my dates, I've found myself thinking, "Take this more seriously! We're talking about creating a life together!" But I've since realized that I have a formal style of meeting, so connecting with someone with a more relaxed manner might be beneficial. Your perception of their initial presentation will depend on your own style of interacting and evaluating.

Personality differences can be advantageous to a parenting partnership. My first partner, Glenn, dresses very casually, and is quiet and shy. I could have discounted him as not being serious or invested in our plans. That would have been a very serious mistake. His personality is very soothing to me, and has added balance to our family. We have been parenting partners for 23 years. Glenn is one of the finest human beings I have ever known, and our son emulates him in all these ways.

Before you conclude that you have a very close match to what you are looking for, you should be in an active getting-to-know-you process with at least three candidates. You should also be spending significant time looking for more candidates. This will give you a multi-dimensional perspective for comparing options and risks. If you're feeling time pressure, you might overlook red flags when you're in the process with only one candidate. Remember to stay fully aware of your "must have" needs as well as your deal breakers. If a potential partner lines up with basic values, continue the courtship until it's clear you're ready to have a child together. Otherwise, both of you should feel free to look for a better match.

You may meet very high quality people with whom you have much in common, and it can be agony to say good-bye. In my search for a third parenting partner I met a lovely bisexual man at a local meet-up group. We hit it off! We could talk for hours, which we did each week for about six months. At the time, I wasn't completely clear about financial resources being one of my top three requirements. I also assumed the candidate was far more solvent than he turned out to be. After all our bonding, we realized we couldn't afford a child together! But years later we are still dear friends and confidants. I imagine our kids will grow up with each other and we will be co-families. Our practical compatibility isn't there, but our affinity is. That said, you might consider a parenting partnership with two or more of your candidates or plan to be co-families.

Expanding your thinking in this way can allow you to keep the wonderful people you meet through your interviewing process in your life. Unlike the search for the one and only soul mate, the search for your parenting partner is enhanced by having more than one significant connection.

***

At this point I need to offer a major warning about projection. Without this warning, you have a high risk of failure in Partnered Parenting relationships no matter how much effort you put in. A great teacher of mine gave me a formula for thinking about other people who have upset me. I asked my teacher, Dr. Pat Allen, how to know if my anger was an unresolved issue from my past. Had I projected into a new relationship, or was there a real issue with the person in question? She replied, "If someone has broken a concrete agreement or has done something immoral or illegal, than you've got an issue with them. If not, keep your mouth shut.

It's your issue to work out some other way. Don't disturb or damage the relationship unless you are sure." Talk about a best practice! It takes discipline to truly consider others through this lens. But treasure those candidates that do not break agreements or do anything immoral or illegal. Those relationships are really valuable.

If you realize that someone is not going to be a good match, be grateful that this was revealed early. Kindly wish that person well. I'm sometimes tempted to give unsolicited advice in those situations. But it's best to give people the space to learn through trial and error. Stay on the karmic high ground with this, and try to leave the person better than you found them. If someone asks why you're turning them down, that's a chance for constructive feedback rather than a harsh critique. You could even give them this book!

Seven: "The Big Ten"

A few basic issues have been at the foundation of my experiences with Partnered Parenting, and I'm sure that's true for anyone who has embarked on this path. There are principles that should be rigorously discussed, negotiated, and planned for by all partnered parents. Let's call them "The Big Ten."

1. God

After many years of talking with men and women about their parenting preferences, I'm surprised how rarely people tell me about their belief in God, or the absence thereof. Has talking about this core issue become so frightening, or such a taboo? If so, I feel that is all the more reason to persevere in creating open dialogue in this area, especially in a negotiation of parenting relationships.

If you have no strong feelings here, you may be tempted to skip the conversation about God altogether. But unless potential parenting partners have expressly told you that religious belief is not an issue for them, initiating direct questions yourself will be the best way to reveal any conflicts or congruencies. Just be gentle and curious in your tone, since it can be a sensitive topic.

Summer, 1998, Miami, Florida. Rachel and Jesse, age 7.

While many people don't have a sense of faith in a higher intelligent force, they may still support that belief in others. This was the case with Glenn, my first parenting partner, who strongly encouraged our son's religious activities. A family's religious diversity can enrich a child's life by widening perspectives, adding choices, and providing greater social awareness. But this can only happen when all family members are committed to finding ways to include and appreciate differing beliefs. Again, Glenn did not relate personally to our son and me going to church activities, but he was curious, honest, and supportive as long as our son was taught to think for himself. Glenn had no need for us to believe as he did, and also had a sincere appreciation for our faith. In this way our differences enriched and added meaning to our lives.

This was yet another way we grew to love and respect Glenn's confidence and leadership as a father and co-parent.

People who are secular or even atheistic in their thinking can still appreciate the benefits of being raised in a religion. I believe that over time the moral and social standards of most religions will promote understanding and connection throughout humanity. I am also confident that the fanaticism and intolerance that exists in some religions is unlikely to be sustained. Humanity is still struggling through a stage of black-and-white, emotionally charged, adolescent thinking. As we "grow up," we will evolve more rational and productive ways to think and move forward. Belief in God – possibly but not necessarily in the context of religion – will have an important role in this process. That's how I feel, and my potential parenting partner might feel differently. That doesn't have to be a deal breaker, but it's something both parties should know about and explore.

2. Money

The amount of money you have to raise your child

will not determine the quality of his or her upbringing, but it is an important factor. Too little money is a hardship and a disadvantage, but vast riches can also bring problems. Planning for and meeting your child's financial needs is both a discipline and a devotion, and it's best to start this process as soon as possible.

As we began to discuss our parenting partnership, Glenn and I agreed that I was best suited to be the primary earner and he would be the primary homemaker. But we would need enough money to sustain my maternity leave before I could go back to work. Unfortunately, we underestimated how long my maternity leave would need to be. We thought three months would be enough, but it turned out I nursed for 3 years! I ended up liquidating my assets to pay for this, and had to rebuild financially when I went back to work.

It was two years before my finances were up to speed again -- just in time to be able to pay for a larger house and private schooling.

To help you avoid that kind of misjudgment, there are several options that have worked for parents in establishing rational, sustainable agreements regarding money.

For example, a "50/50 method" simply divides all expenses down the middle, including emergency savings and future costs such as college expenses. This approach makes sense, provided you can split homemaking and child rearing the same way. I don't recommend this system for people with very different finances and childrearing capabilities. It works best when both partners have equally important careers, incomes, and time for hands-on child rearing. The 50/50 method could also be a good fit if your partnership is using a surrogate, donor eggs, and nannies so you both can focus on career. Or it can work as a second stage plan, after the birthing parent is fully recovered from maternity leave. Full recovery means: her body has healed; she's back in sync with herself, her family, and her friends; and her career and finances are as they were before the maternity leave.

Unless a surrogate is having your child for your partnership, the biological mother will be making the physical sacrifice and taking on the risks of childbirth. For many women this is a total joy, and for others it's a terrifying duty. In any case, gestation and birthing is a tremendous contribution to family building. It can be life threatening and it's always life altering.

In terms of finances, a surrogate typically receives from $25,000 to $50,000 plus all medical and legal costs. Some surrogates also have their food, clothes, and prenatal fitness costs paid as well, which can be another $10,000. Adding the cost of known donor eggs may amount to between $10,000 and $25,000 per cycle.

If the mother in your parenting partnership is becoming pregnant using her own eggs as well as covering expenses such as insurance and her food and clothing, this should be considered her contribution of at least $100,000 to your family. In addition to the $100,000, physicians recommend the baby receive at least a year of nursing/breast milk. This adds another $20,000 or more for just pumped milk. Four months of full coverage infant care could be as much as $40,000. When a mother contributes all the typical things a mother gives to her baby and family, this would equate to $140,000-$160,000 in value for the family through pregnancy and the first four months of your baby's life. In this case, it is fair for the father to contribute this amount as well. This could be in the form of paying for the mother's cost of living and medical bills, or upgrades such as housing and a vehicle that will serve the growing family. If the father doesn't have this financial contribution up front, the agreement should reflect the way he will compensate the family partnership so that things will be fair by the time the child is school age.

There's a simple way to balance this out over time. The father or the father's family can contribute an extra amount toward agreed upon future expenses such as a college fund. Or if you are cohabiting, the father can provide the family home and bequeath this to the children. Perhaps you and your parenting partner can come up with other ideas. The important thing is to factor in the financial realities of pregnancy, birth, and nursing, and the toll these take on the mother. Negotiating these values upfront can prevent confusion in the future. The ongoing costs of raising a child also need cost analysis and planning for the future. You should have a smart, legal agreement fully negotiated before you conceive. Talk with at least two responsible parents who share your lifestyle, as well as an accountant and a child/family counselor, for help with this.

Although it's difficult to separate the parents' hard costs from those of the child, doing so is essential for establishing what the child will need above and beyond your personal lifestyle expenses. Try to agree on a lifestyle cost with which your child will be raised. Then create a separate bank account for the child in order to pay these costs. On a regular basis, both parents should deposit money in this account. If the parents have different earnings, fairness can be achieved by each parent contributing a percentage of his or her income.

To arrive at a well thought out understanding of your family's long term financial requirements, you'll need to define the general level of lifestyle you want and can afford. There's no "right answer" to this. It's just a matter of honestly assessing your financial and emotional realities.

For example, a basic level of childrearing would include shared housing and transportation, the costs of insurance and medical care, public schooling, minimal college savings, minimal paid child care, and a little traveling or other discretionary expenses. I estimate that raising a child in my area of West Los Angeles on this basis would cost $1000-$2000 per month.

A step up from this entails neighborhood housing, at least one car for reliable and convenient transportation, comprehensive insurance and medical coverage, possibly some private schooling and college funding, some paid child care, paid enrichment activities including travel and quality shopping, as well as some savings for other future needs or emergencies. By adhering to a strict budget, I believe the monthly cost of this lifestyle is $2000-$5000 per month.

Beyond this, a still "higher" level comprises a private home, one or more top-of-the-line family vehicles, premium insurance and medical coverage, private schooling, a college fund and/or educational trust, at least three months of expenses in a savings account, domestic help, plus extensive enrichment activities and travel, will cost a minimum of $5000 a month in West Los Angeles and the sky is the limit from there. And remember: spending this kind of money on your child will not improve his or her life if you have to exhaust yourself in order to earn it!

It's worth noting that a significant financial benefit of partnership parenting-- compared to post-divorce co-parenting -- is the option of parenting partners living on the same property. This can provide a higher standard of living while lowering expenses at the same time. In both my parenting partnerships, we had houses on the same property. We shared yards, cars, household needs, and childcare. This arrangement can work, for example, with a house and an adjacent guesthouse, or with a duplex. Apartments in the same complex are another possibility. I will explain the emotional and social advantages of this later in this book.

If figuring income and expense percentages seems too complicated, a simpler plan is to designate a primary homemaker and a primary earner. This will work for most parenting partnerships, especially during maternity leave and the stages of early childhood. If one parent has a demanding career, this method can help protect that career from being disrupted by the ups and downs of family life. The designated homemaker substantially takes charge of day-to-day childrearing. In return, the homemaker should receive an appropriate stipend from the earner. And if the homemaker has given up a career or business to be the primary childcare provider, there should be plans to support the homemaker's transition back to a working life after the child starts school.

Although Glenn, my son's dad, has always had his own business and earned a steady wage, for 18 years I was responsible for providing most of the financial resources. Because Glenn made the day-to-day childrearing a priority over building his personal finances, today he enjoys living at our family home for free. This is the tangible value created by his support for my career.

3. Sex

Where do I start? At the outset, many potential parenting partners assume what the other parent does in the bedroom is that person's exclusive business. It isn't that simple in the real world. What affects one parent affects the child and what affects the child affects the whole family. From the start, some agreements need to be created and respected.

Today there's a general consensus that single parents should wait at least three months before introducing a potential love interest to their children. This getting-to-know-you period can happen smoothly in a parenting partnership, since one parent can date while the child is with the other parent. But what happens when a potentially serious relationship develops in one (or both) of the parent's lives? This needs to be discussed and agreed upon in advance, and made clear in the parenting agreement. You can't anticipate every possibility, but you can talk though common scenarios.

If it comes to choosing between your family agreement and a person you're in love with, you must stick to the agreement. For example, if your love interest is moving away, you could possibly renegotiate your family agreement by asking your parenting partner to move. But if moving isn't feasible, don't break up your family for romantic love. If one parent's romantic interest makes the other parent uneasy – because of drug or alcohol use, for example – a veto agreement can be pre-arranged for this possibility.

On the other hand, if there's no legitimate reason for objecting to a relationship, free choice should be the rule. You should mutually negotiate all this, with equal power and responsibility, when you create your parenting agreement. Sacrifice may be necessary, but you are not just a single adult anymore. You are a child's parent and are accountable for that child's present and future. A love interest may be a chapter in your life but it can also become part of the permanent blueprint of your child's sense of self. If you aren't prepared to "take one for the team" in this area, you shouldn't get involved with a parenting partnership.

The real world details of sex should also be talked about. Will the mother, for example, abstain from new sexual partners while pregnant and nursing? Amid the hormonal changes of pregnancy, many women experience surprising interest (or lack of interest) in sex. Discussion of this before pregnancy is crucial.

And what if the juicy intimacy of having a baby together gets confusing? What if breeding instincts and pheromones kick in, and there is a primal attraction between the parents? I first became aware of this when I was pregnant with my first child. Before I became pregnant with my first child, I felt mostly neutral about sex in general and was not intensely attracted to my parenting partner.

Then, to everyone's surprise, I bloomed into a very turned-on pregnant woman with a wildly instinctual attraction for the person who got me pregnant! This was awkward and inconvenient for both of us until after my son was born and I regained control over myself. It was helpful that my son's dad was 18 years older and patient with me. Back then, I couldn't imagine having a lover that wasn't the father of my child. Today I would certainly accept a trusted lover who was supportive of my parenting partnership.

You may think none of this will happen, but nature

can be tricky.   In my recent search for a new parenting partnership I have become aware that some gay men are romantically and sexually attracted to men, but still have a breeding instinct about impregnating a woman. I first saw this in a man who was deeply in love with his partner of 28 years but told me he planned to conceive their child through natural insemination. I asked, "Would you actually want to have intercourse with a woman?" He said, "I tried it with the last woman we were planning to have a baby with.

It isn't really a romantic or sexual thing. It's more of a primal urge, an instinct to make a baby." You could have blown me over with a feather. Since then, I have encountered this several times.

What if one of the parenting partners meets a true soul connection that doesn't threaten the parenting partnership, and wants to have a child with that person? Ideally, there is support built in to your agreement for both parents to meet a life partner with the intention to expand and blend the family when this happens. A new partner or parent shouldn't be viewed as a threat or a replacement, but another invested adult in family life.

In my parenting partnership now, Paul is like a big brother, gently interviewing my potential love interests and offering insightful observations.

What kind of relationship will develop between your children and your parenting partner's mate? Will they be another mommy or daddy? Or some version of aunt or uncle? You should know that your child will see things from his or her very own perspective. Don't freak out if your partner's girlfriend gets called "my other mommy" or "momma Sarah." Just be confident that no one ever will or ever can replace you as the primary parent of your child.

Finally, I strongly believe that an adult who comes into a child's life has a moral responsibility to the relationship with the child, whether or not the romantic relationship with the child's parent stays intact. My mother had many boyfriends during my childhood and most of them callously dumped me when the love affair ended. I felt helpless or betrayed, and I don't wish those feelings on any child. Fortunately, there were three men who didn't dump me when things ended with my mom. They had the integrity to stay connected to us, and wish me happy birthday and Merry Christmas each year. For decades they have given me advice, help and reassurance. Today I consider them my godfathers, and it has meant a lot to me to know that I was valuable as a person separate from my mother.

4. Education

What does education really mean? The three R's and social enculturation can be provided by public or private schools, but how complete does this seem to you? How well does it align with the values you as a parent want to teach your children? At present there is no agreement across the country on teaching sex education and evolution, or which books should be allowed in school libraries.

Certainly today's kids will need to be familiar with

computers and high technology, but first they need to learn to use their minds, the computers right inside their heads.

The ability to think, to imagine, and to interact skillfully and productively with others is essential. You and your parenting partner have to explore, discuss, and agree on how this will happen for your child. For starters, will there be homeschooling, private schooling, or public schooling?

November 8, 2000, Carden Academy, Maui, Hawaii. Jesse, age 9.

Ironically, "out of the box" thinkers like Glenn and I -- who intended to home-school our child – had a son who was passionate about social order and citizenship. He became an Eagle Scout while attending a college prep academy. When the economy crashed we didn't have money left for college, but fortunately his education was funded and he excelled as a Philosophy major. As for my daughter, she will be able to attend the excellent public schools in our neighborhood. Paul and I expect to have the funds for extracurricular activities and travel, plus saving for college.

At home we make it a priority to discuss concepts such as the origins of life, nutrition and health, and how the world works politically and socially. Asking questions and thinking independently is always encouraged. All parents should consider what education should mean and what education should do. This should be prioritized and agreed upon upfront.

5. Relatives, friends, and your family's future

"Where will we spend the holidays?" That's an important but small-scale question. Here are some larger ones:

"Will there be more kids and how many? Could we add other parenting partners over time?"

"When aging relatives need care, will we take them into our home?"

Even while our kids are still at home, those of us coming into our 40s and 50s are likely to have family members in need. If you accept this responsibility, you will have new expenses related to elder care and you must factor this in to your parenting agreement. Don't get caught in a fight when grandma needs a new wheelchair ramp and your child needs braces. What are you going to do if you can only afford one?

By defining your core values as soon as possible,

you can make the questions much easier to answer. For example, no deliberation will be necessary regarding anyone with untreated alcohol or drug abuse if parenting partners agree about this beforehand. It may seem heartless not to allow a friend or family member with a drinking problem to sleep on the couch. Taking in an elderly family member who abuses prescription drugs can be a wrenching decision. But nurturing your child's stable home life and protecting your parenting partnership must always be your first priorities.

Try to be reasonably flexible about this. During the holidays, your kids may spend time with relatives who don't share all your values. Just don't represent them as role models, or leave children in their care if that seems risky. My second parenting partner's family includes some drinkers, and I certainly am not against seeing them at an annual party. Paul also has someone in his family with an unapologetic criminal background, but I refuse to socialize with him or to allow him to associate with my child. I call this picking my battles.

As a last priority, when you write your wills make sure you agree on guardians for your children. Revisit this agreement each year. Even though Paul has several couples in his family who could be logical choices, we named his young niece who is a single mother with two children. We have confidence in her continuing the values and methods of our partnership, which she has already demonstrated in her own parenting experience.

6. Location

Where will you live, and for how long? Where is your child's primary residence going to be? I strongly believe in parenting partners living no further apart than a "little red wagon ride," and preferably on the same property. I know lots of people are going to want to do it differently, but I can't say the outcome of your child's wellbeing and social adjustment will be the same. Kids need and want both parents every day. They also do well to use their own power to maintain and visit their caregivers without making elaborate appointments to be transported across town. This experience and skill will likely make them responsible and proactive in their relationships for the rest of their lives.

If you choose to live separately than try to keep the continuity of your child's bond to all their caregivers intact and vital. One of the best characteristics of an effective parent is one who facilitates and supports your child's bonds to their other loved ones.

7. Health

Will you have a natural birth at home? Or will it be a hospital birth, and is an epidural okay? Will the child get breast milk or formula and for how long? Will you do vaccinations and which ones and when? Circumcision vs. don't-mess-with-it? Will commercial toys be ok, or will you have strictly not toxic toys. How about diet? Will the child be a vegetarian? Allowed sugar? Fed only organic? Today's health and dietary issues are like religion. Dietary restrictions can become a passionate commitment to not eating animals or animal products, avoiding sugar and gluten or being a full raw food advocate. You need to evaluate these now and decide what priority you will put on this. You and your partner may not have strong opinions about this now, but you might if something comes up, such as chronic ear infections. You will be confronted with tons of differing opinions. Glenn and I started out very strict vegans and animal rights activists and also ate about 75% whole and organic foods. Over the years I became less strict and decided to start eating free range/ organic meat and some dairy. I now believe that it is the success of ethical farms that have the best chance of creating a profit incentive to raise and kill animals humanely, so I support them. I also believe that providing food for human beings is more meaningful existence for an animal than living out a forgotten life. As I do great things in this world, I give the animals I eat a part in my accomplishments. That said, I had to stick to my original parenting agreement and feed our son a vegan diet and respect his father's choices on this subject. Honoring the integrity of the agreement that was the basis for our having our son together was more important than my personal change.

Paul is a vegetarian too, yet we agreed that we would respect each other's choices and let our daughter choose what she will do. We agreed that the main concern we share is good whole nutrition for our girl and to role model this.

Food may not be an issue, but fitness and activity levels can be. Paul and I have ongoing discussions about this because I have a core value of health and fitness. I believe it is unethical to be really out of shape and unhealthy while raising a child. It is an avoidable risk that will dramatically increase your chances of getting diseases more often and sooner. Being out of shape also reduces your quality of life, vitality and life expectancy. Is it fair to ask your child to come into your life and worry about you, or have to watch you suffer? I feel strongly that modeling unhealthy eating and a lack of fitness to your child is unethical. Kids hardly have a choice in emulating you. Do you really want them to spend their lives struggling with the consequences of being out of shape? Less energy, health, fashion choices, confidence and choices in mates is a big price for them to pay for your lack of discipline.

Will there be drinking in moderation? Will your kids be allowed to take a sip? You and your parenting partner have to agree on this especially if either of you have a family history of alcoholism. Is sugar and caffeine ok for kids? Or will you regard these as drugs?

What is the amount of sleep that children should have? I admit this is one of my parenting flaws. My son's dad was very strict about bedtimes that allowed our son to sleep at least 9 hours a night. He insisted on this for proper brain development and a strong immune system. He was right and all the studies are coming out to confirm this. I have bad habits about this and so does my daughter's dad. Sadly, our daughter is getting short changed. I am really working on it, but you may want to learn from my mistake and put agreements about sleep in your agreement.

Sun exposure is another issue. Are you going to use sunscreen or plan your days around shade, hats and timing? Since the UV from the sun is so damaging, it is an issue to consider. I for one, wish my mother didn't let me burn every year of my childhood since this is now showing up in my skin today. I never had a choice! My dermatologist agrees that it is your child's right to not be damaged this way.

Without becoming neurotic, it is important to think through health issues as a serious ethical concern with long-term outcomes. Like the old adage "measure twice and cut once," planning is a discipline that will pay in immeasurable ways.

8. Time

Time is irreplaceable. Your child will only be a child for a short amount of time. Believe me, they are babies for a year, blink, and they are going to school; blink again and they are teens struggling for independence. How you negotiate the time you will have with your child will determine many things. And yes, love to a child is spelled TIME.

One reason I like Partnered Parenting better than single parents sharing custody, is that the time you can spend together will be more rich and meaningful to everyone, especially the child. You will find that children naturally want all their caregivers together with them as much as possible. They love to hold both their parents hands and swing and much more. Since children do not have the cognitive ability to feel individuated from either parent until about 16, they will feel that everything the parents direct at each other, is directed at them.

Love, time, caring, fun, and affection between parents are all ways your child will feel about his or herself. I know for some this is not what you had in mind when you thought of Partnered Parenting, but I am here to tell you what your child will experience so you can make child-loving choices for your time negotiation. Consider agreeing to at least one dinner and weekend day all together each week. Also agree on how holidays will be spent. As much as possible celebrate annual traditions together so your child feels the added security of the landmarks of time's passing. This is the main way a child understands time – similar event to similar event spent with loved ones.

If you are living apart or on the same property, there should be a sense of peaceful daily routine for the child. Ideally the child sees both parents every day. If you are going to be a work focused parent and not around for most of the child's day to day activities, try and do a bed time ritual like brushing teeth and reading books. Believe me, you and your child will benefit in the long run from this touchstone of time. Many child psychologists will tell you that children who feel they can count on a parent will be less likely to test a parent with power struggles and bad behavior later. When you're out of town, use Face Time or Skype to maintain that predictable connection.

You can easily build your other activities around this sacred time especially if you choose a parenting partner who is supportive of these scheduled times. Make sure this is in your agreement.

If you are going to live apart, you can divide the time in different ways. Many people find it easier for the child to be at one parent's house through the weekday routine and the other on weekends. Especially at school age, the child will benefit from not having disruption when keeping track of homework and school clothes.

In my first parenting partnership, Glenn was mostly in charge of the day-to-day school and weekly activities with me supplementing. Glenn was better suited for this structured routine than I. However, when it came to social planning, adventuring and trips, I was in charge of this. Even though I saw our son every day and had weekly family dinners together, weekends were my main connection when outside the weekday routine. Before Jesse was conceived, Glenn and I discussed this as the best way to do it, and sure enough, it worked great.

9. Discipline

By what method will your discipline the child and how will this change at the different stages of your child's development? Will you be using time outs? How long will the child be allowed to have a pacifier or bottle? How will you teach a child to not yell or hit? Sibling rivalry might be an issue if there will be other kids in the home.

Both parents must cultivate the skills to discipline without being abusive or ineffective. There are many great books on the subject with time-tested methods. It might be good to go online and take a look at the top styles of parenting and their techniques, such as counting to three, a board with happy face stickers to track progress, rewards vs. punishment, etc. Another reason I recommend the Foster Care training is that it does teach effective discipline that seems to have the best outcomes for kids especially in complex family situations. Foster Care training can also help clarify how you were disciplined -- bringing to light both negative and positive effects. Without a conscious choice to learn new ways to do things, we will end up disciplining our kids the way our parents disciplined us. I was abused and neglected as a child, so I had to read tons of parenting books while pregnant and practice, practice, practice, to be ready for parenthood. In some ways this was beneficial to feeling I had to create a clean slate in our parenting partnership. We both agreed on doing things different than our parents and together helped each other establish discipline standards that worked.

 The main thing is to be on the same page with your co-parent. Your styles of parenting in general can be different, but correcting and disciplining your child should be as similar as possible to be effective. The child needs to be able to predict the effects of his or her behavior to feel competent in meeting your expectations. This consistency of direction, will also eliminate the child from playing parents against each other.

Life can be complicated and we humans are imperfect. I have slipped up and yelled at my kids in ways that I wish I had not. The ghosts from my childhood often rear their ugly faces through my own mistakes. My parenting partners knew I would have these challenges before they parented with me and they worked hard to support me in my efforts to overcome this. You can form a similar alliance with your parenting partner. You can count on them and they can count on you.

10. Community and Home Life

Although I love and respect conventional marriage, I knew that basing my child's home life on the shifting sands of love and intimacy were not right for me. It's not that my love is inconstant, it's just that I am not a true pair-bonder, but prefer to be a member of a community. I have been blessed with several very healthy and loving romantic partnerships that would have easily become thriving marriages (some of these suitors still want to marry me). It's me that just doesn't fit the coupling mold. For one thing, collaborating with an extended family and community in raising kids feels like good human resource management. Several heads are better than two, and many adults invested in the lives of children can be better than even the most dedicated loving couple. At least it's been this way for me.

Jesse's birthday party, January 2000, Maui Hawaii. Jesse is in the red shirt, center. Rachel is second from right, back row.

It is never too early to be loyal to your future unborn children! Although having a bunch of mommies is not a bad way to grow up, having a consistent father figure too is the preference of many people. Sure, life happens and we can't control the other parent, but you do get a choice with whom you conceive. The first way to love your kids is picking their other parent(s) with their best interests in mind. My choice of co-parents/fathers of my children hasn't always been smooth, but it has certainly been a success.

Glenn and I lived on the same property for most of the twenty years of raising our son, and although our son is on his own now, Glenn and I are still dedicated to each other's well-being and are the best of friends. He lives on my property in Hawaii. I feel I got all the best parts of being in a 23 year marriage, without the stress of dimming sexual attraction that so often leads to people going numb or replacing each other. I didn't want to take that chance since I'm still not sure if I have any choice to whom I'm attracted and for how long. Maybe it's a chemical cocktail Mother-Nature brewed up to get us to trust strangers quickly and make babies?

How do I make a community? It's tricky when our individualistic American culture has fierce independence pumping in its heart. I am as unique and self-sufficient as they come, but I feel that I and my children thrive in an intentional, community home life. I strive to balance cultivating my personal passions and purpose in life with contributing to the people around me in tangible ways. Yes, it's sometimes uncomfortable to allow people to depend on me, and to allow myself to depend on others. What if someone fails? That could and does happen.

For example, Paul and I had challenges based on our living in different states while parenting our toddler Grace. Today we all share a home (something we thought we'd never do) and because of this our daughter is thriving. Also living with us are my best friend Hannah and another friend, Alan. We are a tribe, more than housemates, sharing expenses, childcare, meals, laughter, dance, art supplies, cars, chores, sorrows and victories. Hannah or Paul brings me breakfast at my computer most mornings. Alan takes the cars in for service and is always ready to fix the computers. Me, I just oversee the big picture of where and how. In other words, I pay for most of it and allow everyone to contribute what he or she can.

Many people think this is idealistic, and indeed it is. We count on each other and that's one reason it works. It's sort of like getting in shape because you have a gym buddy that you don't flake on. I believe that there is such a need for this that it will work! "Necessity is the Mother of invention!"

"Social innovation" is happening in our home. Raising children with lifelong tribal bonds is fulfilling and meaningful for us. I am proud of us for pioneering this modern family option.

Eight: Red flags when considering a Parenting Partner

Negotiating a parenting partnership means dealing with several different perspectives. You're customizing the relationship in consideration for the needs of the child, taking into consideration the abilities and circumstances of the parents. That said, you still need to be alert for red flags throughout the entire process. When looking through on-line profiles and evaluating potential partners in your circle of family, friends and colleagues, look for these red-flag indicators. Don't waste your time with a lot of getting-to-know-you correspondence that will lead to disappointment. If you don't see these negative indicators in the beginning keep this checklist in mind. Anything else you can think of that is illegal, immoral or unethical should be clearly seen and dealt with. One advantage of getting to know a potential parenting partner versus a romantic partner is that you will be less likely to be blinded by your attraction or discount red flags because you are in love and feeling inspired by an almost magic sense that things will just work out. Hint, this is Mother Nature's cocktail to get you to make as many babies as possible regardless of whether this is a sensible, healthy or sustainable choice. She doesn't care; she is going for high numbers of births for human survival and doesn't really care how fulfilling your family is for you or your children.

If a person has not demonstrated a proficiency at basic self-care and management, they are not ready for parenting. Watch out for women on line who want to get pregnant in order to be taken care of. Being provided for during maternity and while the child is little isn't manipulative. It's good planning and in the best interests of the child.
The problem is when a woman has never provided

for herself and is looking for a way to stay dependent on someone else. If the mom doesn't have a certain amount of maturity and self-reliance, she will be selfish with her kids or use them to get her needs met that she should meet herself.

I noticed many men on websites looking to become a father without any financial responsibility. If this is what everyone agrees to, and there are other money sources to let him off the hook, so be it. My concern is, if the only financial source is the mother and something happens to her or her ability to earn, what will happen to the child? Will society have to pick up the slack? This doesn't seem fair when you should be making a rational rather than an emotional choice. Please consider a father who at least is willing and able to step in and provide if needed. Or get creative and ask grandparents or godparents to sign legal documents taking secondary responsibility. The point is, kids need at least two parents who can and will provide if needed.

It is true that many people who aren't ready can get ready very quickly when a child is on the way. But an even larger number of people don't or can't sustain consistent parenting long enough to get kids raised. So, since you are making a rational and planned choice, you can choose to get to know people who support themselves financially; eat and drink in moderation; and make and keep agreements that allow them create and sustain relationships and good social standing. They also should clearly abstain from behavior that society and insurance companies consider high risk. If it is too risky for an insurance company to insure, it is too risky for your child's essential parent.

Untreated illness and addictions are huge red flags. Shame and denial are two symptoms that make it more difficult to see these problems early on. If a potential parenting partner is overweight enough to be a health hazard, they could have a food addiction, which is serious, since being overweight will take years of your life and dramatically increase your chances of illness. Plus, like alcohol or smoking, children are very likely to emulate the parent's behavior.

If people haven't mastered basic routines of self-care - such as regular meals, domestic and personal hygiene, and common sense safety, as well as paying bills, fulfilling work and social obligations in a timely manner - they will have a very hard time administering the basic routines kids need to stay healthy, safe and emotionally secure. Children need feeding, bathing, clothing, playing, socializing, learning, affection, attention, stimulation, challenge, opportunities, freedom and safety every single day. Parents are responsible for providing this and making sure that their child receives this reliably in the future. If a person can't do this for himself or herself, they are not yet qualified to be a partner for parenting.

A chronic history of bad credit and of not paying

debts or keeping promises will likely continue into the future unless it is clear that the issue was related to a specific time like divorce, lay off, the economic crash or illness. This can be verified with a full credit report since old history will show good standing until the specific event and then good standing again.

Criminal backgrounds are not necessarily a deal breaker in my opinion. It all depends on the crime, and when and how it was dealt with. I know plenty of good parents who have a lot of street sense and wisdom to teach kids because they spent time in jail during their youth for things like one-time marijuana possession or spray-painting graffiti. To me, a red flag is an on-going issue with the legal authorities and anything violent or perverse. You might want to ask about their whole family and anyone who could have access to children. Like many families, both my parenting partners and I have people who have perpetrated sex abuse on children.

If you eliminated all families who have this issue, you might eliminate about half the world or more.

It's best to bring it all out into the light and agree on a strategy for prevention. In my parenting agreements we have allowed no contact with perpetrators or those who did not, knowingly, render aid to children who were abused. It might be hard to draw this line, but worth it. Going through this difficult terrain with your potential parenting partner will be revealing too. If they are too nervous or reluctant to deal with this in a competent way, it is a red flag. These days, protecting your children and teaching them self-protection from violence or premature sexual exposure and experiences is part of the necessary skills to be an effective parent. We live in a concrete jungle where there are predators. Like looking both ways before crossing the street or not getting in a car with a stranger, how not to get molested is something you have to be able to discuss as parents, with family and eventually with your kids.

It is perfectly valid to do a background and credit report on a potential parent. Don't think it's rude or intrusive if you are on your 4th or 5th "date". You wouldn't waste time in escrow buying a house or doing a business merger without basic verification.

The same thing applies with making a conscious choice for making a family, only more so.

Foster parenting is another good way to bring all these things into the open while also getting a great education for parenting. The shared training a good way to get on the same page quickly. You will naturally find red flags, and possibly more than you could think of on your own. Do you want to parent with someone who the state would not certify as a foster parent? Also, you may find the process so rewarding that you might plan to have a foster child placed with you. Since the laws have changed requiring kids to be given permanent placement within two years, you have a good chance of being offered the option to adopt as well. This wouldn't necessarily take the place of having kids of your own. I am a foster mom because it has been tremendously rewarding to care for kids in need, and has helped me grow in my ability to really connect with the needs of kids and collaborate better with the other caregivers who are involved.

If you ask most people why they want to have children they will tell you that it is to fulfill their own wishes and needs. If this weren't the case, the human race would have died out long ago. It might be a good idea to ask people why they think they are ready to become a parent. What skills and resources they have to give to raising children? They may still say something like "I just want kids so much I will figure it out as I go" or "I have love and attention to give." Don't jump on their case. Just know that they are in an immature stage of desire to be a parent and are still growing. For these people, it may be good for them to start with being an auntie or uncle, volunteering for Big Brothers Big Sisters, or foster parenting with a team until they have a more developed sense of the needs of children.

Along the same lines, if someone tells you that they had a nightmare childhood and want to have a child to do it differently than their parents, or they want to have someone to shore up their life as with an heir to carry on a legacy, this isn't necessarily a red flag unless that's their only reason. These two ideas are common and can be strong motivators to be good parents. These are only red flags when the person cannot say how a child, the other parent and the world will benefit from their having children. For example "I want to be proud of my kids. I feel I am a patient and good instructor who will teach my child how to be a responsible and valuable member of society." Or, "I understand that kids need to feel they can really count on their dad to be consistent and do what he promises. My dad wasn't and I know how that feels so I will be especially careful to provide a solid foundation for my kids."

Nine: Fertility - How will you make the baby?

There is so much to know about fertility and fertility medicine. I have extensive experience with the Southern California Reproductive Center (SCRC), which I see as a perfect model of what a fertility center should provide. It's a great resource for both information and leading edge clinical care, including alternative therapies.

I strongly recommend visiting SCRC's website, where you can find everything you need to know about reproductive medicine. For our purposes here, I'll concentrate on the areas that are most likely to be of interest to partnered parents.

I want to jump to In Vitro Fertilization (IVF) because it can stop the clock – which is a major issue in parenting partnerships. If you have selected your parenting partner and negotiated an agreement, but you find you need more time to finish school, change your job, deal with an illness in the family, buy a house, or save more money before conceiving, you have some options.

You and your partner can use IVF to make embryos and freeze them. These embryos do not deteriorate while frozen, so this buys you time without your body added risks to the quality of your eggs or sperm cells.

Another advantage to freezing embryos is the testing and screening for abnormalities that can be done. This will reduce your risk of having an atypical pregnancy and child. With age and environmental exposure, the egg and sperm cells will take on more and more defects that can devastate your family. Dramatically reducing this risk is worth the upfront costs in my opinion. For men and women becoming parents in their late 30's and older, I can't recommend it enough. My family and I used pre-conception genetic testing, IVF and embryo chromosomal testing. We have tremendous gratitude for the peace of mind and planning advantages it gave us.

While the benefit of IVF is stopping the clock, the drawback is this: "frozen people" means you're locked in legally and genetically with your parenting partner. Besides the cost and extra difficulty, another drawback to IVF is you may end up with embryos in cryo-freeze. There is a complex moral and legal responsibility that comes with this. No matter what your religious beliefs are, these embryos are created for a hope at life. You have to be on the same page with your parenting partner on these moral issues or you are going to get into trouble. If you end up with three embryos and decide to only have two kids, what will happen to the third? Adoption? Used by another family member? Donation to research? Disposal? Please think this through with a counselor before starting.

But even if you have a counselor and an agreement, things can go awry. Paul and I both needed IVF in order to conceive our daughter, and it was a success our first try. We also brought into being a frozen male embryo we named Samuel. He is a five-day-old fully formed blastula. You might think that this tiny cluster of cells is just tissue, but to us he has all the same potential that our 5 year old daughter has. Every day that Grace runs around voicing her unique opinions about life, I think of her tiny, fraternal, frozen twin. The technologies that are available for conception should not distract you from the real human experience of bringing a child into the world.

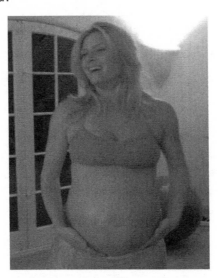

December 2008, Los Angeles. Rachel dancing through labor, a few hours before Grace's birth.

If you are under 35 the cost/benefits ratio for egg freezing could make sense for you and buy you time to do more planning and preparing for your family. This doesn't mean you can't do future rounds of egg retrieval and make embryos, it just gives you some eggs put away if you need more time to pick the right parenting partner for getting pregnant or making embryos. If you are the would-be father and you have an old friend or family member who is willing to give you eggs, this is a way to receive these eggs, freeze them, and then plan ahead for your family at a later date.

Our sperm or eggs are best before the age of forty years old. I know I may be a little overly enthusiastic, but I tell all the young people in my life to freeze their eggs and sperm. This is as much an investment in you future as college or savings. If it's hard to afford when you're young, ask your parents to help. They might be very happy to make sure they get healthy grandkids someday when you are settled and successful!

Ten: Legal Issues

As with marriage or with any other contract, the law does not protect you from itself. You are accountable for what you do, and being ignorant of legal ramifications will not shield you from the consequences. With regard to newly emerging realities such as surrogates, anonymous donors, known donors, and parenting partnerships, law is being formed by the cases brought to court, and that will be changing and reshaping for decades to come.

An attorney once told me, "The law only works for people who care about it." With this in mind, you should make every effort to draft a parenting agreement in the form of a legally binding contract, but an agreement is only as good as the people who sign it. Verify history, facts, and intentions, and get good at holding each other accountable as your primary means to enforcement.

Hiring a lawyer to legalize your contract is not a foolproof solution to enforcing your agreement. Courts are full of people who are not keeping their legal agreements. That is why they are there. Hiring a lawyer should be regarded as the way you declare your intentions to the legal system, and willingly ask that system to hold you both accountable. It is a public declaration similar to a marriage with witnesses.

If you can afford it, you can use a law office as a kind of escrow to gather documents and verification until both parties are satisfied. This can help to keep things very clean and minimize confusion. This is the same role that the escrow on a home purchase fulfills. The documentation for a parenting partnership will be more like the information given for a property purchase, business merger and a prenuptial all in one! It should encompass credit reports, health history, full financials, legal history, verification of life insurance, clear title to assets, mental health, expected costs and budgets for having and raising the child, and your well-negotiated agreement on who is doing what in your partnered family.

Have a conscious intention to avoid ever going before a judge. If you do go before a judge, you are in effect saying that you have failed to resolve your issues by yourselves, and now turn final decision over to a person in a black robe. You will actually give up your right to make important decisions regarding your child. Do not get to this point! Don't give up on working things out for yourselves and don't think that Big Daddy will solve everything for you.

Here's an idea to help you with creating your agreement and holding yourselves accountable. Choose someone, or several people, to act as your resolution committee. Ask them to act as arbitrator if you should fail to come up with a resolution yourselves. They will go through your agreement with both of you and make very sure they know what it is you are doing and agreeing to. This way they can help to enforce it. If it comes to renegotiation, an interpretation of the original intent will have to be determined so the new agreement can serve that original intent as best it can. It would help if there are people available – other than the legal authorities – who can mediate the process of organizing emotionally charged issues.

Don't think in terms of protecting only your rights. You should be just as invested in protecting the other parent's rights as your own. By doing so, you protect the children's rights to have both parents caring for them and loving them the best they can. You should always look for ways to build up your parenting partner and never exploit their weaknesses and failures for personal gain. Ultimately, that would only cost your child. You must protect your child and yourself from illegal, immoral and unethical behavior, but do this in a proactive way that seeks to restore harmony and functional family life as soon as possible.

Never react in a punitive way. If you do, everyone will lose.

Finally, here's a very important practical note. Getting pregnant these days can happen in a number of ways. The best practice for a parenting partnership is to use a clinic even if just for basic insemination. If you conceive outside a clinic, you are under state and federal law which will not uphold much of your parenting agreement. If a doctor initiates the pregnancy, than the unique laws regarding a third party conception will be in effect. The law is already well established regarding the variations of known donors and gay and lesbian parenting. As long as your attorney says your agreement is legally binding, the agreement should be upheld as long as you conceive through a doctor or clinic. This is very important. For a full explanation of this and all other legal issues mentioned in this section, consult an attorney in you state.

Eleven: After the birth - alternative parenting

Having a baby together is a very intimate experience between two people. Even if you think your parenting partnership is not romantic or sexual, the intimacy of sharing a new life can arouse some of these feelings. Hopefully, you have talked about this and have prepared to work this out rationally and patiently. For a mother it is important to understand that the baby you are carrying wants to hear the voices she's heard in utero after she is born. She wants her kin around her from the day of her birth.

The time directly after the birth should be a time with many people helping to care for the baby and seeing to the mother's recovery from the exhaustive ordeal of birth.

When Glenn and I moved to Maui I was pregnant and we had few friends. We became very bonded. He helped deliver our son in a home birth. We shared a family bed for several months after that. He would do diaper changing and rocking to allow me more sleep between nursing. The organic nature of this made me confused for a while and I had a strong attraction for him. I wanted affection and intimacy he was not prepared to give. We got through it and after I recovered and our son was able to be away from the breast for two hours at a time, I began to date a very nice single dad who was a supportive and helpful addition to our lives. This was a win/win all around and put everything back to normal between Glenn and me.

With Paul, I tried to avoid the blurred boundaries. I had a hospital birth. Paul arrived after the birth to see our daughter and then went back home to Portland. I then did my postpartum recovery at a small studio apartment with the help of many devoted friends. We would all pile into my big king size bed and watch movies and eat snacks. They did my laundry, shopping and dishes. This community of loved ones really gave even better support than I had when it was just Glenn and I with a newborn. I really do believe that it takes a village to recover from childbirth. And, in the case of a parenting partnership, the group dynamic can help with not becoming overwhelmed by the intimacy and intensity of having a child together.

Having said that, I also believe it's hugely beneficial for babies to be with both the mother and father as soon as and as much as possible.

I believe children come out of the womb hardwired to hear and smell their parents and family who will be there for them the rest of their lives. I wish Paul and Grace had had a better bonding early on, and I often wonder if some of her intense testing of him is a result of this. She seems to need almost constant reassurance that he is here and loves her.

December 2012, Los Angeles. Rachel and Paul with
their daughter Grace, age 4.

Do the work during the pregnancy to establish
strong bonds with friends and family that will see
you through the birth and early infant care. You
don't want to be sorting this out after you already
have a wiggly little person in your arms. I met some
really wonderful friends I still have today at prenatal
yoga. As I write this, one of the most supportive
people who championed Grace's birth and our

recovery is sitting near me editing what I write.

Inclusion is key, but so is discernment. Be prepared to set excellent boundaries with people who might be disruptive. Even friends and family you normally connect well with have to be reevaluated. Sometimes people are curious and pushy, especially when you have an alternative family. They want to spectate and amuse themselves without truly investing care and time. Be prepared to politely decline those who approach you this way. Empower your parenting partner to guard you and your child from well-meaning and yet misguided people. Teamwork and watching each other's back is a beautiful benefit to parenting with a trusted partner.

The birth of your child is a vivid time that is a critical for setting the theme and tone for your family life. These early experiences can follow you for many years. Take care to be at your best and don't allow yourself to say or do anything to damage your relationship at this very vulnerable and memorable time. Work to facilitate both parents' relationship to the baby.

As you parent for the eighteen or more years together, reflect on these bonds and develop a steadfast devotion to your child. Be a champion team for your child and never let anything get in the way of this primary commitment and bond. Children are totally dependent and at the mercy of your choices and you owe them your devotion. Your child's wellbeing cannot be separated from either parent's wellbeing, so your concern, respect and love should extend to them as well. Good luck with this. In the real world of human life, parenting is supposed to be a challenge. Every difficulty you overcome will make you stronger for facing the next one. Get help from counselors, spiritual guidance, parenting classes and plenty of family meetings.

Twelve: A kid's perspective on his partnered parents

Many people ask how our alternative family life affected our son, Jesse. His father and I took a big risk 23 years ago when we created our parenting partnership agreement. We really didn't know what would happen. Jesse might have felt embarrassed for himself, alienated from us, or teased by others. We hoped that the benefit of having stable, constant parents who would not "break up" would compensate for whatever hardship he'd have to endure.

Our decision to home school Jesse might have been influenced by our desire to shield him from any rude reality until he was old enough to understand our reasons for deviating so far from convention. Meanwhile, our family seemed quite normal at our park play-group, beach socials, and birthday parties.

When Jesse was seven, he insisted on going to school with other kids. He wanted to be a regular kid, and he also wanted the order and structure of a rigorously academic school, uniforms and all! Glenn and I knew our son was growing into a unique individual, and maybe a little rebellious toward his parents' outside-the-norm ideals. We sought to support him in this, and also help him cultivate acceptance for changing social systems, differing lifestyles, and diverse cultures. "Teaching moments" regularly presented themselves in the melting pot that was and still is Hawaii.

I remember the day we had a "special talk" with Jesse shortly after he had started school. We asked him how he felt about our family and about our being different from the other families we knew. To our surprise, he had already caught on to our reason for asking.

Our normally soft spoken son launched into a lecture I will never forget. He said, "Different? You don't know how nuts it is over at my friends' houses.

All their parents are fighting and breaking up. That's why we are always over here. You guys are so nice to each other." At that moment, Glenn and I realized that this was about more than just our little family. Maybe we were doing something that could help other people too? Maybe this parenting partnership option could help prevent divorce?

There isn't a lot of information about kids' outcomes when raised by alternative families. In addition to being a small demographic, it's still hard to isolate information about intact alternative families as a contrast to broken ones. In a New York *Times* article in June of 2012 titled *Debate on a Study Examining Gay Parents,* the writer outlines the struggle to show conclusive data about kids with Gay parents.

Although Glenn and I are not gay parents, one point in the article does validate the main reason we chose to co-parent. This was our commitment to avoiding divorce. We had both grown up in divorced families, and we had also been affected by divorces in most of the families around us.

I'm certainly in favor of making families that are more divorce resistant, and doing everything else to serve the best interests of parents and kids. I'm proud and grateful that Jesse has been an outstanding student, an Eagle Scout, and a contributing member of society. As it happened, Glenn and I had the joy of giving our son what we ourselves did not receive. It's very healing to feel we somehow figured out a way to make a custom-designed family work.

Summer 2002, Maui, Hawaii. Glenn and Rachel with their son Jesse, age 11, at Boy Scout camp.

Made in the USA
San Bernardino, CA
25 April 2015